The National Tramway Museum

In the beginning there was no time and no place. Just men with a mission and a desperate desire to rescue, store and restore as many trams as possible during the "Termination Terror" of the 1950's.

Truly men of vision – for the trams return. By stealth or with a fanfare, trams are coming back on track – but those at the National Tramway Museum are the originals!

This award winning "Museum on the Move" has gradually been developed to become one of the finest transport Museums in the country, and if you haven't visited for several years – you must! It's a continually changing and ever-fascinating place.

The National Tramway Museum, Crich, Derbyshire. Tel: 01773 852565

Copyright ©1995 text and design Milepost 92$^1\!/_2$

This edition first published 1995 by Milepost Publishing in conjunction with
Arcturus Publishing Limited and exclusively for Bookmart Limited
Desford Road, Enderby, Leicester, LE9 5AD

Milepost Publishing is a division of Milepost 92$^1\!/_2$,
Colin Garratt's Audio Visual, Photographic and Picture Library for the Railway Industry

Designed by Milepost/Wilson Design Associates
Originated, Printed and Bound in the UK by Gresham Print Group, Nottingham

ISBN 1 900193 20 5

Milepost 92$^1\!/_2$
Newton Harcourt
Leicestershire
LE8 9FH
Tel:0 0116 259 2068

MILEPOST

TRAMS
OF SOUTHERN BRITAIN

MILEPOST

INTRODUCTION

Some of Henry Priestley's journeys south to photograph trams were only just in time, for tramways were abandoned early in many places. So he recorded the tramways of Bath, Bristol, Merthyr, Reading and Coventry, all of which ceased running before or early in the second world war.

This section also includes some of his London and Birmingham pictures, and a tribute to the many vistas offered by the Llandudno & Colwyn Bay line. London with the complexity of its conduit trackwork provided many subjects for his camera, both north of the Thames and south, while Birmingham pre-war offered contrasts between the city's own main roads and the tortuous routes it took over from the Birmingham & Midland company.

Was it the weather that led to so many smaller towns in the south to use open top tramcars? Did the absence of heavy industry give a clarity to the atmosphere, as well as leaving buildings less covered in grime than in the northern cities? Whatever it was, Henry Priestley used the same techniques of photography, looking for a high vantage point, sun shining across the tracks, movement and animation in the street scenes, and always plenty of detail.

Here too, you feel you can almost step into the picture. And why not?

Everything about this scene speaks of elegance, whether the mid-1890s styling of Bristol Tramways and Carriage Company car 123, built by Milnes in 1900, or the celebratory scrollwork adorning the tram stop sign, or the April 1939 fashions of the ladies alighting from the tramcar in Ashton Road. Fashion drawings at this period depicted ladies of unbelievable slimness, but the diet of the time tended less towards weight than that of today, and the average height of people was slightly less. The Belisha beacon speaks of growing motor traffic, though the road is still relatively empty, and metal studs rather than zebra stripes mark the crossing on the road surface.

Previous spread

So much of the tramway story is caught up in this London Transport car, recorded by Henry Priestley on the corner of Camden Road and Caledonian Road in July 1938. Built by Brush in 1909 as Metropolitan Electric Tramways class H car 238, it has been updated in various ways before becoming London Transport car 2170 in 1933. It is running on the centre slot conduit current collection system of the former London County Council lines, but already the overhead wires are in place for trolleybuses that will replace tram route 59 in October. Throughout 1938 there were fears of war, leading to the Munich meetings in September, and already in July the sign on the Tufnell Park Garage appeals for volunteers for the Air Raid Precautions service. Meanwhile the limousine with gleaming hinges to its folding top forges ahead; the tramcar will turn left, crossing behind it.

Core of the vast London tramway network was the former London County Council system, much of which had centre-slot conduit current collection instead of conventional overhead wires. Cars of class E3, built in 1930-31 with metal bodywork to run through the Kingsway Subway, are seen on route 31, *top left*, from Hackney to Battersea and Wandsworth in July 1938, while *above*, ex-Metropolitan Electric car 2196 pauses for traffic lights alongside Dorothy's guaranteed Perms on Seven Sisters Road near Finsbury Park Station. Overhead wires in both pictures are for the new trolleybuses. South of the Thames, HR2 class car 1887 modernised in the 1930s along with many E1 class cars, swings through the Blackheath Hill loop on Lewisham Road, *bottom left*, in September 1951.

Llandudno & Colwyn Bay Electric, with all its timeless elegance. Have the couple just alighted from ex-Bournemouth car 15 at Benarth Road, *top left*, to look at a prospective home for their retirement? Will they consider the trams, the lattice pole and the shelter made out of old tramcar bulkhead doors, as assets to the neighbourhood? Some of those doors came from cars like number 17, seen entering private right of way, *bottom left*, on the Little Orme. Both these were taken in August 1954; in September 1953 car 15 at Maesgwyn, *right*, leaves the section of single track made necessary when the sea eroded the track on the right. This was a private toll road belonging to the tramway company.

Over page

Plymouth built its last new cars in 1926-27, and this car, 166 seen at Peverell in August 1938, was the last of the batch. Originally on bogies, most, like this one, were later mounted on a four wheeled truck. Its styling, advanced in the mid-1920's, was quickly overtaken by the jazzy styles epitomised by the lady on the left. And also by the new double deck buses.

Not all London's streets are wide, and other traffic has to squeeze past the trams. On Camden Road approaching the High Street, ex-Walthamstow 1927-built car 2048, together with E1 1156 and two buses, *above*, pose a problem for the learner driver in the sports car in June 1938. Another close squeeze for E3 car 202, one of those built in 1931 for Leyton, *top right*, running on overhead wires at Leytonstone Church in July 1938; signal lights for the single track ahead are on the pole on the left. At Highbury, *bottom right*, E3 car 1949 in June 1938 passes a Luton-head van of the type originally designed to carry light but bulky loads of straw hats, while the Highbury Fish Restaurant offers generous helpings for ninepence.

White-gloved police constable directs traffic in Colwyn Bay in May 1953, *above*, including two Crosville buses and Llandudno car 2, still with its Accrington bogies. In Birmingham, *top right*, a white macintosh coat makes the policeman on duty readily visible at Saltley where the Washwood Heath and Alum Rock routes divide. 798 and 789 are Brush-built air-braked cars of 1928-29. Same distinctive uniform for a constable at the Summer Row, Birmingham, *bottom right*, as Smethwick-bound car 196 heads into Sand Pits Parade. The bow-collector equipped car behind is on route 32 and will turn into Newhall Hill.

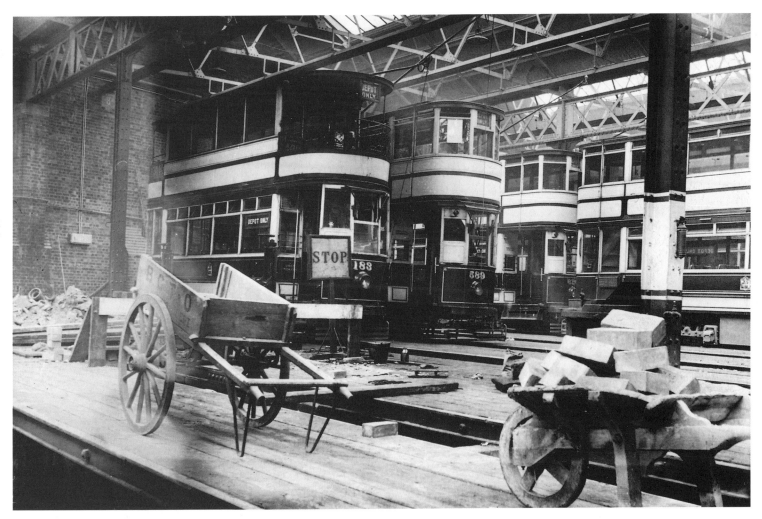

So often in a tram depot there was a feeling of Marie Celeste mystery, of tasks left half-finished by unseen engineering staff. In Merthyr Tydfil's depot, *left*, built on the site of the Penydaren Ironworks, Henry Priestley lets us look in April 1938 through the windscreen of ex-Birmingham car 6 at ex-Birmingham & Midland car 15 and car 5, one of Merthyr's original single deck fleet of 1900, piled high with spare seats. In Birmingham, *above*, he takes us into the far corner of Hockley Depot in March 1939, only a few weeks before it ceased to house trams. The handcart's inscription BCT&O refers to Birmingham Corporation Tramways & Omnibuses. Balcony car 183 of 1906 became one of those stored as a strategic reserve fleet in wartime. Cars 589, 626 and 510 date from 1920-21 and continued in service on other routes.

Over page

How London's conduit system filled the street surfaces with tramway ironmongery! At York Road terminus, Wandsworth, in April 1948, the points have been set in both running rail and conduit for 1931-built E3 car 205. The trolleybus wiring here vanished at the same time as the Wandsworth route trams in 1950. Over the wall on the left is Young's brewery, and today this is known as Ram Street.

In June 1939 Graham Road, *top left*, shows London Transport in transition. 1907-built E1 car 881 is flanked by an open staircase bus and a bus of the latest STL variety. A trolleybus flashes past, and a 1920s taxi has just been hailed. In April 1939 in Birmingham, *bottom left*, car 102 picks up passengers on Dudley Road at Icknield Port Road while a mother attempts to cross the road with a pram. In August 1939 Cardiff car 31, *top right*, enters the single track at Hayes Bridge, and in the same month Bedworth-bound Coventry car 66, still only a few years old, approaches the Burges junction, *bottom right*.

It is August 1953, and Llandudno ex-Bournemouth car 14 has a good load of passengers at the Mostyn Street corner, *left*. A well-loaded open top car always looked like a window-box full of flowers. Motor car registrations indicate that Llandudno has visitors from Caernarvonshire, Manchester and London. And the Crosville bus on the left looks like an early Leyland TD1, already over 20 years old. Looking in the other direction towards the West Shore terminus, *above*, a boy tries out his bicycle across the tram tracks in front of ex-Accrington car 4.

Birmingham 634, built 1921 as a balcony car, slows for Short Heath terminus in April 1953, *top left*, where a modern No Entry sign is lit by a gas lamp. Years later, this was the site of a short-lived guided busway. At the Gravelly junction, *bottom left*, Birmingham 647, one of a 1923-24 batch by the Midland Railway Carriage & Wagon Company, heads towards the city in September 1937. Two months before final closure in 1953, car 543 heads through the back streets near Miller Street Depot, *top right*.

Over page
Car number 8 of the Merthyr Electric Traction & Lighting Company's fleet was built at the Birmingham & Midland Tramways' Tividale Works, sometime between 1913 and 1916. Merthyr bought it in 1929, and here Henry Priestley takes a child's eye view of it in Penydaren Road in April 1938.

A succession of railway bridges provide a stage-like setting for trams. Cardiff low-height car 100 vanishes beneath the former Taff Vale Railway bridge near Queen Street station, *top left*, in September 1937. Excursions advertised include one to Oxford, including lunch and a visit to the Morris car works, all for 12s 6d, or 62^1/$_2$p. Beneath the shadows of Wandsworth Town station bridge, London, *bottom left*, E3 car 203 of 1931 swings left on to double track to catch any motorist unawares in June 1949. Orthochromatic film not only records the red of the trams and trolleybuses as solid black, but also the amber top of the belisha beacon. Today this area is pedestrianised and gentrified. And *above*, back to Cardiff for the other side of the Taff Vale bridge with car 101, the prototype Brush low-height car of 1923. Henry Priestley had to get special permission to photograph from here; he is standing on the ex-Rhymney Railway bridge over Newport Road, this time in August 1939.

Leicester 144 at the Clock Tower in June 1937, *left*, with Stone's pointing the way forward with its television sign. Traffic jostles trams here, and also *above* in Coventry's Broadgate in August 1939, with cars 58, 50 and 53 bound for Stoke and Bell Green. Bomb damage the following year and subsequent rebuilding have changed Coventry's centre almost out of recognition.

Over page
An animated scene to delight the heart of Henry Priestley, at Park Street on the boundary between Grimsby and Cleethorpes, in April 1937, during the three months when Grimsby had converted its part of the through route to trolleybuses, but Cleethorpes had yet to do so. Car 57 originated with the Great Grimsby Street Tramways Company, which sold half its line to Grimsby in 1925 and the remaining two miles to Cleethorpes in 1936. New trolleybus poles are going up in the background, meanwhile the road is thronged with people changing from trolleybus to tram.

In postwar London suburbs the photographer could be an object of curiosity for small boys whose tailored jackets, coats and caps, along with short trousers and long socks, give a flavour of the period almost as much as the trams themselves do. Rebuilt 1910 E1 car 1396 is reversing at Battersea Bridge approach in April 1950, *above*; disconnected tracks curve into the riverside permanent way yard. At Greenwich Church, *top right*, another rebuilt E1, car 985 of 1907, has just arrived in April 1949. The Addington Street triangle, *bottom right*, was one of the last new pieces of conduit trackwork laid in London. Visible through the gap in the buildings in April 1950 are the platform canopies of Waterloo Station; a British Railways ex-LMS six-ton Scammell mechanical horse is parked on the left. The small boy in the Daniel Neal of Portman Square topcoat is far more interested in the newly-laid mass of steel in the street.

Parked cars and bicycles fill up the space between trams and the kerb in Leicester in May 1938, where *top left* cars 106 and 152 pass at the Great Central Street junction, and *bottom left* car 59 pursues a cyclist while number 76, now preserved at the National Tramway Museum, waits at traffic lights in Granby Street. Humberstone Gate, Leicester, *top right*, offers three tracks, three tramcars, an underground lavatory and a motorist about to do a U-turn. In Cardiff in April 1938, *bottom right*, Gladwins' truck has plenty of room to park while passengers board Brush-built lowheight car 98 at the Tudor Street/Clare Road junction.

While repairs to the sea wall continue at Maesgwyn, Llandudno ex-Bournemouth car 7 runs on the wrong track, *top left*, and slows to regain its proper track via the crossover. In August 1954 Llandudno car 5, one of five bought from Accrington in 1931, makes the descent of the Bodafon Fields right of way to regain Llandudno streets at Craig-y-Don, *bottom left*. The shelter names the stop as Nant-y-Gamar. At Maesgwyn in August 1955 work on sea defences is well advanced, but the seaward track is covered in sand, *above*, while well-filled car 10 heads for Llandudno, bathers head for the beach, and Henry Priestley records the view from an ex-Bournemouth open top car waiting its turn for the single line.

Henry Priestley took the *top left* view near Kingswood terminus, Bristol, on a wet August day in 1938, "just to show the interlaced track". Car 124 is scarcely altered since it began work in 1900. The cyclist takes good care to keep clear of the tracks on this rain-burnished road. In July 1939 Birmingham bogie car 714 of the 1925 series, *bottom left*, has just come up from Gravelly Hill to Park Road junction and the driver is setting the points to turn towards Witton depot.

The pattern of road surfaces and tracks shows up *above* at Lodge Road terminus, where bow-collector equipped Birmingham car 61 of 1905 stands in July 1939. Poster hoardings and tramcars were often the only spots of bright colour in a soot-laden urban landscape.

Over page

At nearly 20 points on the London tramways, change pits were provided to allow cars to change between centre-slot conduit and overhead current collection. Men like these twin brothers at Mile End Road in June 1939, top, lined up the "ploughs" ready to feed them into cars entering the conduit section, using the two pronged fork. E3 type car 190, one of those supplied by London County Council in 1931 to run the Leyton tramways, heads gingerly forward, still on overhead power, past some track repairs. There was always an overlap of conduit and overhead wiring at these change pits, and cars in the other direction would stop immediately before the change point to raise the trolleypole, then accelerate past. The end of the conduit, diverted across the running rails into the pit, would bring the discarded plough bouncing out on its own, always a fascinating operation to see.

The cool and quiet of a tram depot, and those unforgettable smells of gear oil and freshly dried sand. In May 1937 Henry Priestley uses the bulkhead of Coventry car 35 to record open top car 34 in Priestley's Bridge Depot, *left*, but for open top car 31, *above*, he set up his camera on a car step to give a maintenance man's eye view. The wall rising on the right is actually the lower or 'rocker' panel of a tramcar, viewed at close quarters.

Henry Priestley often chose high vantage points, and here at Bristol he excels himself. "I wanted to get that trolley standard," he says, and in April 1939 he records 1895-built car 125's top deck, and beyond it, approaching the Bedminster Parade loop, *top left*, is car 7 of 1900. "I wanted a picture of someone boarding. And that lovely centre pole carrying four wires." And he succeeds, this time in April 1938, with a young lady boarding a car at Old Market, *bottom left*, with trolleypoles disclosing two more cars in front and car 166 about to leave for Nags Head Hill Top. Open tops did not disappear with Bristol trams in 1941, and a boy watches quizzically as Henry Priestley stands to take a picture on Llandudno ex-Bournemouth car 13 at Colwyn Bay terminus, *above,* in August 1953. One of these cars is preserved, restored to its Bournemouth colours. But for twenty years they were synonymous with Llandudno and Colwyn Bay, and part of the elegance went with them.

A London E1 car emerges from Church Crescent, Hackney, *top left*, flanked by new, heavier poles planted for trolleybus wiring. On the Lauriston Road corner, the shop, shut on this Sunday in June 1939, carries advertising for six different brands of cigarettes. Cardiff car 70, reversing at Clarence Road terminus in September 1937, *centre left*, stands alongside a poster announcing Paul Robeson and Cedric Hardwicke in King Solomon's Mines. Not forgetting Idris at the organ. A close look at the *bottom left* picture in Leicester, taken outside the Great Northern station, shows that a flock of sheep is holding up car 92 and other home-going Wednesday rush hour traffic in May 1938. In Birmingham, *above*, bogie car 723 negotiates part of the complex layout of one way street workings in the Cannon Hill area at the Court Road/Edward Road junction in April 1938. Betts, gents outfitter, offers Swallow raincoats at 30s (£1.50).

Brighton, more than just London-by-the-Sea. Until 1939 its open top tramcars, many newly-built, ran on a cluster of 3ft 6in gauge routes radiating from the Aquarium. In August 1934 locally-built car 26 pauses on Queen's Road, *above*, in front of a splendid church built of flints, while Durtnall's removal truck pauses to make a delivery. In April 1939, *top right*, Birmingham 1906-built car 93 passes a Stop-me-and-buy-one uniformed ice-cream man with his tricycle outside the Grove cinema. A year earlier, Cardiff car 14 picks up passengers in Cathedral Road, *bottom right*, as evening shadows lengthen.

In London, *above*, Henry Priestley climbs to the balcony of a block of flats to record E1 class car 558 of 1930 in Tooley Street at Tower Bridge Road, in August 1949. The car has two trolley bases but only one pole; fortunately route 70, like much of inner London's tramway network, is entirely on the centre slot conduit system. Bristol ran 1895-style open top cars from start to finish; car 26, a Milnes product of 1900, swings past Bedminster depot into West Street in April 1939, *top right*. Birmingham 88 of 1906 passes Victoria Park, Smethwick in the same month, *bottom right*; children in these pictures will be in their sixties now.

Merthyr Tydfil had three single-and-loops tram routes totalling 3 ½ miles, and a fleet of 14 trams, 13 of them second hand. Car 14, *top left*, at Dowlais in April 1938, was bought in 1929 from Birmingham & Midland Tramways. The destination, following B&MT practice, is displayed on the front bulkhead. In July 1938 London E1 car 601, last of the 1930 delivery, loads in Goswell Road at the Aldersgate terminus, *bottom left*, flanked by butchers' delivery cycles and a milkman's hand-propelled 'pram'. And in December 1938 a Bristol motorman, well wrapped in greatcoat and gloves, waits at Colston Avenue while passengers disembark, *above*. Did the ladies with fur wraps travel upstairs? Locally-made signs direct to Bath and Gloucester, but a modern car park sign has appeared, left.

Henry Priestley had seen this Coventry car with an extended destination display and caught it from the top of another, waiting for 51 to clear single track in Stoney Stanton Road, *above*, in May 1937. Coventry car 69 passes the tramway siding into Bell Green station yard, used for delivery of tramway materials, *top right*, in August 1939. Cardiff 23, rebuilt in 1920 from a 1902 model, enters single track in Cowbridge Road, *centre right*. White bands on poles and blackout masks on headlamp and street lights denote wartime; the picture was taken in August 1940. Birmingham car 107 passes the entrance to Tividale depot and works, former Birmingham & Midland headquarters, *bottom right*, in April 1939. Tracks and wires still lead in to the works for power supply purposes.

Stepping out into the road to board a tram in Reading in July 1938, *top left*, near Wokingham Road junction. Overhead fittings for trolleybuses are already visible and the linesmen's tower wagon is parked on the left. Reading's trams ran on 4 ft gauge tracks and this 1903 car was rebuilt in the 1920s. In the same month Henry Priestley photographed London E1 car 907 at Forest Rise at Whipps Cross, *bottom left*. Tracks to the left lead to reserved track along Whipps Cross Road. *Above*, Birmingham balcony car 341 waits for passengers at Selly Oak on a wet day in September 1937. Tramwaymen stand around the Bundy time recorder clock and over the road the church advertises its harvest thanksgiving services.

Previous pages
Moving to the east side of the ex-Rhymney Railway bridge (see earlier page) Henry Priestley records Cardiff car 60, one of the final 1924-25 batch of low height cars, heading towards the city centre along Newport Road a few weeks before the outbreak of the 1939-45 war. Would anyone today push a child in a pushchair across a main road at so acute an angle as the young lady on the left?

Birmingham was at the centre of a vast network of 3ft 6in gauge tram tracks, stretching out into the Black Country towns. *Above*, Birmingham car 808, dating from 1928-9, moves up to the Navigation Street loading point during the last weeks before the Bristol Road routes closed in July 1952. Also on 3ft 6in gauge was the Llandudno & Colwyn Bay Electric Railway; mainstay of its fleet in later years were ten elegant open top cars, secondhand from Bournemouth in 1936. Car 13, 1921-built, *top right*, heads along Penrhyn Avenue in August 1954, while sister car 12 is seen from another open top on Mostyn Street corner, Llandudno, *bottom right*, surrounded by taxis, visitors' cars, and the local council's sightseeing bus fleet.

Over page

As well as being the work of a noted tramway photographer, these pictures have benefitted from the specialised photographic processing facilities of the National Tramway Museum. Photographic archivist Glynn Wilton had to give a series of seven different exposures to bring out the various details of this view of Bath Electric Tramways, taken in September 1937, and many other pictures in this book have required similar care in printing. So, with clarity we see every part of the scene as two of the elegant single deck cars pass on Bath Old Bridge; in the distance an open top car turns towards the Great Western Railway station and the pinnacles of Bath Abbey show above the rooftops. All these cars date from 1904, were built by Milnes, and wore a distinctive livery of bright blue and primrose yellow. A bamboo pole with a hooked end is carried on the side of car 51 for use in dewirements or turning the trolleypole at intermediate terminal points; automatic reversers were provided at most termini and the open top cars had ropes. Buses took over in 1939.

Cyclists show the speed of the photographer's exposure as they blur across the tram tracks. In Coventry, *top left*, car 61 has just negotiated a short piece of interlaced track in Bishop Street in August 1939. Two Birmingham bogie cars pause at the Grove Lane junction with Soho Road, *bottom left*, in March 1939, with notices in their front windows of impending conversion of all the Hockley Depot-based routes to buses on 1 April. Seconds later, a fast-moving car from Dudley or Wednesbury would have filled the lens. At Washwood Heath Depot stop, *above*, bow-collector-equipped car 810 takes up passengers while a builder's Fordson truck demonstrates overtaking a tram on the offside.

Conversion of north London tram routes to trolleybuses was in full swing in July 1938 when Henry Priestley recorded E1 car 1193, one of the 1908-09 batch, *top left*, at Woodford Napier Arms terminus on the edge of Epping Forest. On the poster hoardings, Clark Gable and Myrna Loy in Manhattan Melodrama, and 84,000 new members joined the London Co-op in 1937. In Bristol, *bottom left*, posters for Kodak film as well as the cinema form a background at Nags Head Hill Top in April 1939 to car 124, little changed since it left Milnes' works in 1900. Advertisements swathe the buildings at the corner of Pentonville road, Kings Cross, *above*, as London car 536 emerges from Grays Inn Road one Sunday in June 1938; this is not an E1 but the earlier E type, dating from 1906.

Plymouth staff called the 1924 batch of tramcars "square faces"; the angular English Electric lines of car 133, *above*, show in this 1938 view at the Guildhall. Conduit track but no overhead wires at Tooting Broadway, London, *top right*, in March 1950, where the conductor of ex-Walthamstow 1927-built car 2045 watches the pointsman on the pavement pull the lever to bring the car round the curve. Compare it with the smooth asphalt road and neat overhead wiring at Selly Oak, Birmingham, *bottom right*, where in September 1937 Rednal-bound balcony car 358 waits for car 396 to clear the crossover. Today much has changed at this scene, but the University tower remains in the background.

Over page

Birmingham had already abandoned several tram routes when it opened this section of reserved sleeper track along Sutton New Road in September 1938 to by-pass the narrow Erdington High Street. In May 1953, only a few weeks before the final closure of Birmingham tramways, pedestrians cross with confidence in front of car 563, and already the white stripes of a zebra crossing and an international pattern of no-entry sign point the way into future years. The striped end-blind of the shop, and its end wall, tar-painted for weather protection, are features of the period. And there is not a single television aerial in sight.

Traffic and tramline: A limousine overtakes Reading car 24 on the offside while the tanker lorry, restricted to 20 mph, hangs back on the nearside at Sussex Place loop, Wokingham Road, *top left*. It is July 1938; trolleybus fittings have already been added to the spanwires. In London, *bottom left*, E1 car 949, running on trolley, is about to cross the Mile End Road conduit tracks to reach Burdett Road in June 1939. Another London picture, *top right*, this time with orthochromatic film, shows well turned-out HR2 car 1860 of 1930 in Lewisham Road at John Penn Street. Cyclists overtaking the parked Dennis Pax truck will need to avoid the tram tracks.

Previous pages
Shirley Temple tops the bill at the cinema and trolleybus wiring clings like ivy to the tram wires at Greengate, West Ham, as London Transport E1 car 1296, new in 1910, pauses on its way from Barking to Aldgate in 1938. Boards on the side of the tramcar advertise cheap mid-day fares as well as giving route details.

Leicester 59 pauses at the end of Groby Road in June 1937, *top left*, before turning left on to the Abbey Park Road reserved track and so to the depot. A fine display of deck chairs at the corner shop. Car 169 loads passengers outside Leicester Midland station in May 1938, *bottom left*. A bamboo pole for turning the trolley is hung along the bottom of the car side. With camera held low, giving a child's viewpoint, Henry Priestley captures a crowd of workers boarding city-bound Birmingham car 148 outside West Smethwick Depot, *above*. This B&MT depot was used by Birmingham from 1928 till the last trams ran to Dudley in 1939.

Scrapyard scenes at St Denys, Southampton, *top and bottom left*, in June 1949 when the remaining trams there still had six months to run. The low-built open top cars, with their back-to-back 'knifeboard' seats on top, were designed to fit under the medieval Bargate arch, later by-passed. The balcony cars worked on other routes. One of the open top cars, no. 45 is preserved at the National Tramway Museum and others are being restored locally. Bristol Tramways created their own scrapyard by knocking a hole through the back wall of Kingswood depot and laying tracks into a field, *above*. Car 57 of 1900 is one of about 20 cars Henry Priestley found there in August 1939, following closure of the Zetland road routes in July. Piles of tramcar seats lie to right and left of the picture.

In June 1949, London is still busy healing the scars of wartime bombing, with temporary single storey shops in many places. Trams have been overhauled and their new red and cream paintwork is a bright spot in street scenes of austerity; any new buses available are needed urgently to replace worn-out pre-war buses. London Transport car 552 dates from 1930, one of the final batch of E1 class cars built with bogies and equipment from single deck cars which worked the Kingsway Subway routes till it was deepened to take double decks in 1930-31. Growth of road traffic is such that Henry Priestley would today find it difficult to take up this position for more than a few seconds in the middle of Waterloo Road, looking towards St George's Circus. The Old Vic theatre is still there on the left, and trams seem set to reappear in Croydon, once part of the great London network.